Wild About Guitars

Inspiring, effective teaching resources

Ruth Wild

Easy Level

Acknowledgement from the author

I would like to thank Mark Lippert, for his invaluable specialist input. Also, Stephen, my husband, for his considerable practical and moral support.

ISBN: 979-8-8428-3550-8

© August 2022

Design: riverdesignbooks.com

Contents

Introduction: The Thinking Behind
Wild About Guitars

Independent Learning

One of our most important objectives as teachers is to enable our pupils to develop independence. What does that mean exactly for instrumental music teachers, and how will this book help?

The list below shows the characteristics of independent learners in the context of instrumental music.

Independent instrumental music learners:

- **can listen for themselves, think for themselves, make musical decisions (create), so that:**
    - they have a clear idea of an intended sound, recognise if they have played a sound other than that which is intended, and understand how to adjust it accordingly
    - they consider the effects of playing something in different ways, and form opinions about what sounds better
    - they can make up their own musical material using the notes they know how to play
    - they are able to learn music in different ways, including with and without notation

- **can adapt to:**
    - playing in different situations (such as a new band/ensemble)
    - playing in different sound worlds, such as music from different periods or genres

- **are motivated to:**
    - attend the next lesson
    - improve
    - practise between lessons
    - attend an ensemble/join a band
    - carry on playing when they leave school

I am sure that we can all recognise these attributes as beneficial for our pupils. Our role as teachers is vital in helping pupils achieve them.

We need to:

- enable pupils to listen and think for themselves, and to make musical decisions
- nurture pupils' curiosity for different sound worlds and equip them with the necessary musical tools
- ensure pupils are motivated: understanding and addressing any social and psychological issues that may affect their willingness to try something and to pursue it.

Wild About Guitars contains activities that encourage learners to listen and think for themselves. Aural activities are largely played on the instrument, and wherever possible use real music – pieces rather than exercises. As most activities are played on the instrument, they are particularly effective in encouraging pupils to listen and evaluate their own playing (including, for instance, spotting when they have played an incorrect pitch, and self-correcting). I have included non-notated activities, which provide opportunities for pupils to focus more on listening and less on looking. This means that their attention will be more easily directed towards the evaluation of their own playing. Activities also help learners to make musical decisions – these come in the form of improvising, interpreting and arranging.

Wild About Guitars will help you provide pupils with a good foundation in a comprehensive range of skills, including aural, creative, and notation. Pupils will develop their ability to learn music in different ways, be it from notation or without. This will enable them to participate in a diverse range of ensembles. They will learn to play both melodies and chords, ensuring the foundations are laid for playing in different styles, and for taking on different roles in groups.

Wild About Guitars will equip you to teach pupils an ensemble piece without notation. This will allow them to be more receptive to their fellow musicians. By regularly playing without notation, pupils will increase their aural awareness, developing their capacity to absorb stylistic differences between music of different periods, places and genres. This book will ensure that your pupils have the necessary musical tools to explore and enjoy a range of sound worlds.

Wild About Guitars will help pupils realise that they are making progress. Experience has shown me that all pupils have the potential to enjoy learning and performing music in different ways. It is true that pupils sometimes appear in the first instance to have less aptitude or motivation in a particular area. However, this is often due to a lack of self-belief; they attribute a perceived lack of success to something about themselves that they can't change. Activities from this book will gently guide them through the different ways of playing music in easy step-by-step stages.

Wild About Guitars has detailed explanations of how to teach the activities. We as teachers may feel under-confident in a particular area of making music – be it playing *with* notation, *without* notation, or improvising. With this in mind, I have described the activities clearly and simply, with many 'Points to Note' and 'Top Tips.'

Learning Through Playing

The activities in **Wild About Guitars** are mostly played on pupils' instruments. Using the voice and body percussion can be very helpful, and some activities include these strategies. But in weekly instrumental lessons, often the best way to develop generic musical skills – general musicianship - is through playing. The reasons for this are practical, musical and educational, as shown below:

- Holistic learning. Musicians need to listen and create *whilst* playing. The activities we use with pupils need to reflect this. It is useful to remember too, that technical skills may be developed and consolidated by carrying out well-chosen aural and creative activities on the instrument.

- The suitability of the music. Specific characteristics of a piece of music may lend themselves more readily to playing than singing.

- Psychological or physiological problems pupils have in relation to singing. Some pupils may find it more comfortable to play.

- Pupils want to play. In the context of instrumental lessons and ensemble rehearsals pupils' primary motivation is playing their instrument.

- Practicalities. Instrumental lessons are often short. Learning aural and creative skills through playing is normally a better use of time.

Real Music Making

One of the best things we can do to motivate learners is to ensure that there is real music making in every lesson. Pupils love to feel that they are participating in music making where the primary purpose is to express and evoke emotion. Even at an early stage, learners are aware that a piece can be musically satisfying. Therefore, activities in the book are as far as possible pieces of music rather than exercises, games or warm-ups - including those concerned with general musicianship - for example, aural and creative activities. Aural skills are developed by working out pieces by ear, or learning pieces by rote. Creative skills are developed by interpreting and arranging pieces, and by creating melodies. Improvising is made to feel like proper music making, even with beginners, by the use of attractive backing tracks.

How to integrate the activities with pupils' other learning

Pupils need to learn and develop a broad range of skills. The best way to do this is simultaneously, with no skill left behind. In WCET[1] and ensembles, where sessions normally last a reasonably long time this is relatively straightforward. However, in individual and small group lessons this can be daunting. Given that lessons are short – often no more than twenty minutes - you may worry about how to include aural and creative activities. Will technique be neglected? How will activities fit with a pupil's tutor book?

In *Wild About Guitars*, I give advice about how to use the activities in lessons, bearing in mind time constraints, and that the natural flow of the lesson still needs to happen: hearing what has been practised; helping the pupil to develop and consolidate skills; preparing the pupil for subsequent practice. I indicate where activities are better used as parts of lessons – in which case I recommend how to divide up the learning – and where they may be used to cover an entire lesson.

Activities are centred around key stages of learning: when the first two notes and one finger chords are learnt; when a pentatonic and a two finger chord can be played; when a scale and a three finger chord can be played. This means that the technical matters associated with these stages can be developed and consolidated - for example, changing from one string or chord to another can be practised, not only by a piece from a tutor book, but by using the activities from the first section of *Wild About Guitars.* As activities are largely played on the instrument, this increases the opportunities to hone technical points.

It is clear which notes are used in the activities. This ensures that it is easy to determine which stage of a tutor book they correspond to.

Notation activities will improve pupils' ability to read pieces from their tutor books.

[1] Whole Class Ensemble Teaching – or 'Wider Opportunities'

What Can We Do with Two Notes and One Finger Chords?

Activities use strings **B** and **E** and chords **C** and **G7**

For backing tracks visit:
www.musicwild.co.uk
and go to the
'Wild About Guitars' tab

Activity 1: Echo Playing

see audio links '1a)i) and 1a)ii) Echo Playing 2 notes – E and B'*
and '1b)i) and 1b)ii) Echo Playing 2 chords – C and G7'*

- Play phrases of 2 bars in 4/4 using strings E and B for pupils to copy back.
- Repeat the activity using chords C and G7.

*tracks labelled i) include phrases for pupils to copy back, so facilitate home practice; tracks labelled ii) contain just the backing, giving the teacher more flexibility in lessons.

Point to note:

Activities for chords can be returned to at a later date if that is preferred.

Top tips:

- Tell pupils which note/chord your first phrase will start on. You may wish to use just one note/chord for your first phrase.
- Be prepared to repeat a phrase if a pupil isn't successful first time.
- Ensure pupils work out the notes with aural clues not visual – ensure they can't see your fingers by standing behind them, or by asking them to face different parts of the room. For single strings you can also sing the notes, or turn your guitar around so that the back is facing them.

Supplementary exercise for differentiating pitch.

Some of your pupils may not yet believe they can differentiate between pitches: the idea is too abstract for them – they haven't yet learnt that their ears can give them the relevant information. If this is the case, follow the steps below:

- Demonstrate what we mean by high and low in music by showing some extreme examples – a very high note, and a very low note.

- Play one string repeatedly then change to an adjacent one (e.g. B to E, or E to B). Ask pupils to show that they have spotted the change in pitch with a hand gesture – simply low hand for low pitch, high hand for high pitch. Repeat, ensuring that pupils are using their ears, and not following any visual clues, such as from your instrument, or from another pupil. You can do this by standing behind them or asking them to face different parts of the room. Alternatively, you can turn your instrument around with the back facing them and pluck the strings.

- Pupils will easily recognise the change in sound, and this will help them realise that they can recognise changes in pitch.

- As pupils improve at this, oscillate between the two pitches, becoming more rapid for greater challenge, and to add fun, though never exceeding pupils' ability to accomplish the task.

Activity 2: Improvising - Riff and Rest, Riff and Play

see audio links '2a) Riff and Rest 2 notes - E and B' and '2b) Riff and Rest 2 chords - C and G7.' A 'tutti' phrase is included.

- Decide on a 2 bar phrase in 4/4 using the strings E and B, or the chords C and G7. Teach it to your pupils aurally. (See examples on pages 11 and 12.)

- Ask pupils to play the phrase, then leave a gap of the same length, then play the same phrase again, in other words: 2 bar phrase, 2 bars rest, 2 bar phrase. Do this on a loop. Pupils can count 1 2 3 4|1 2 3 4 for the bars' rest, or use fun words such as hot po-ta-to, hot po-ta-to. Pupils' own names, food or animals might be sources for the words.

- Importantly, learners now need to internalise that phrase length. Ask them to repeat the actions in the last bullet point, but now counting in their heads, not out loud. Then ask them to repeat with no visual clues from you or their fellow learners. They might, for instance, turn to face away from each other.

- Next fill the gap with your own improvisations, choosing from the same notes, and demonstrating at least some improvisations that are very simple – perhaps just a rhythm on one of the notes/chords and some rests. Learners are now playing the phrase all together, listening to your improvisation, playing the phrase all together, and so on.

- Ask learners to fill in the gaps with their own improvisations. They will now be playing the same phrase all together, followed by their own improvisations, followed by the same phrase all together. Continue to do this on a loop (over and over). It is good that they get more than one chance at improvising. In a group practising chord improvisations, you may wish to use one chord at a time to avoid clashes of pitches, though if the group is small enough, and confident enough, you may wish to go straight into individual improvisations.

Top tips:

- The process can be broken into small chunks – perhaps a bullet point or two at a time - then returned to the following lesson.

- You don't need to use the term improvisation specifically. 'Make up your own tune' or 'pattern' will suffice with less experienced pupils.

- Remind learners that simple improvisations are often the best, and that they only need to use two strings suggested. Choosing even just one note at this stage is fine. Practising rhythms on one chord at a time is desirable if performing group improvisations, as mentioned above.

- You should always join in with the 'tutti' phrase (the one they all play) at the right time – exactly after two bars has elapsed, even if some pupils seem to be over- or under-running with their improvisations. It is vital that the sense of pulse is maintained and that learners continue to internalise the correct phrase length.

- If you have a group, start to ask smaller numbers of learners at a time to improvise. In a class or ensemble situation you can split pupils into small groups by, for instance, asking what they had for lunch. Those who had sandwiches can do the first improvisation, those who had chips can do the second improvisation and so on. Next ask if any pairs of pupils would like to improvise together, and finally ask for solos. Avoid going down a line asking for solo improvisations in a large group – it can be quite stressful waiting for your turn!

Example:

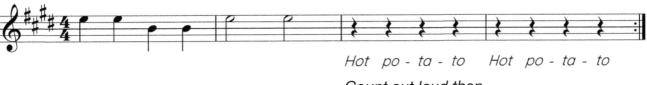

Hot po - ta - to   Hot po - ta - to

Count out loud then....
Count in heads then.....
Count in heads no visual clues

Next.........................

Teacher improvises...............

Hot po - ta - to   Hot po - ta - to

Then...............................

Pupils improvise.....................

Hot po - ta - to   Hot po - ta - to

Example for chords:

Count out loud then….
Count in heads then…..
Count in heads no visual clues

Next………………………..

Teacher improvises……………

Then…………………………..

Pupils improvise…………………..

Hot   Po   ta - to   Hot   Po - ta - to

12

Activity 3: Working Out By Ear

- Sing the first two bars of Old Macdonald Had a Farm, starting on E, and ask pupils if they have heard the tune before. (If not, other tunes containing a leap of a perfect fourth such as London's Burning or Auld Lang Syne (starting on B) can be used.)

- Sing just the first three notes, and ask pupils whether or not they are all the same. Sometimes pupils are confused because the words of the song are different, so feel that there has been a change of pitch too. If that is the case try playing the first three notes, standing behind them so they can't see your fingers and instrument (pupils need to work this out aurally, not visually). They will normally then realise that the three notes are the same.

- Say that the first note is an E, and establish that therefore all the notes are E.

- Now sing or play the first four notes. Ask if the fourth note is the same as the first three or different. When pupils have established that it is different, ask if it is higher or lower than the first three notes*.

- When pupils have established that the next note is lower, ask them what it could be. Ask pupils to try out their suggestions so that they can confirm whether or not their answer is correct.

- Once it is established that the next note is B, all play the first four notes together.

Top tips:

- *If pupils are finding it difficult to differentiate pitch, use the supplementary exercise under Activity 1: Echo Playing.

- Always ensure pupils are working out the notes aurally, i.e. without visual clues.

- If second finger is known, carry on with the next three notes using the same process.

Activity 4: Learning a Tune Without Notation – Bear Dance

see audio links: '3 Bear Dance; 3i) Bear Dance guitar one; 3ii) Bear Dance guitar two; 3iii) Bear Dance guitar three; 3iv) Bear Dance guitar four.'

See score for Bear Dance on p.16. For pupils playing two notes refer to the fourth line of the stave.

- Explain to pupils that for this piece, their shoulders will be B and their heads will be E. Ask pupils to tap their heads in time, whilst saying E E E E, then tap their heads followed by shoulders whilst saying E E B.
- Next ask them to tap and sing those notes - E E E E E E B.
- Then just tap, whilst singing the notes in their heads.

Say/sing/sing in heads	E	E	E	E
Tap	head	head	head	head
	E	E	B	
	head	head	shoulders	

- Play those notes with your pupils.
- Use the same procedure for the next four bars: saying and tapping; singing and tapping; singing in heads and tapping; playing.
- Repeat each four bar section as necessary, and once pupils can remember the notes easily, add the two sections together. For the crotchet rests, the instrument can be tapped, and this can be retained for performance purposes, or transferred to 'thinking voice.' Play through the eight bars a few times.
- Ask pupils to play their part whilst you play the tune (line 1 or line 2). Sometimes pupils find it easier to tap their part first whilst you play the tune.
- For bars 9 to 12 use the same procedure but use the words 'beans on toast' to help internalise the rhythm – 'beans on' for the two quavers, 'toast' for the crotchets… So, tap and say, then tap and sing, then tap and think:

14

beans on	toast	beans on	toast
E E	E	B B	B

beans on	toast	toast
E E	E	B

- Play bars 13 to 16 to pupils - some may notice that they are the same as bars 5 to 8. Once pupils are confident playing bars 9 to 12, and bars 13 to 16, join the sections together. Again, a tap may be used for the crotchet rests. Play several times.

- Ask pupils to play their part whilst you play the tune.

- Revise the beginning and play all the way through.

Top tips:

- Unless pupils have access to a recording of the music it will be difficult for them to practise the material at home. If that is the case devote a comparatively small proportion of the lesson to learning the piece and return to it the following week. This will ensure you have enough time to spend on what **will** be practised for the following lesson.

- You can also ask pupils to think of their own words for the rhythm in bars 9 to 12. Ask them to choose a theme, such as food, pets, football teams and film characters. Tap the rhythm and see if they can think of some words to fit.

- Using the same principles, arrange your own pieces to suit your pupils.

Bear Dance

Supplementary rhythm/ensemble exercise for subdividing the beat:

- Ask pupils to choose words of one syllable and two syllables. Food, pets, football teams and film characters are good themes. The one syllabled word will be used for crotchets and the two syllabled word for quavers.

- Start pupils off playing crotchets on a B string, saying the word simultaneously. Whilst they are doing that play quavers on the E string, again saying the relevant word.

- Swap roles so that pupils now play the two syllabled word whilst you play the one syllabled word. They will now be subdividing the beat into quavers.

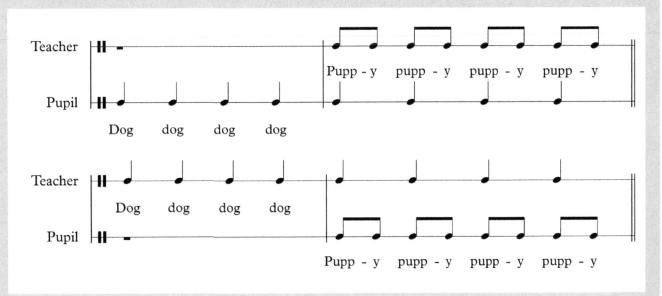

Top tips:

- Let pupils try and work out the correct speed of the quavers themselves, and only intervene as necessary. Advise them not to come in straight away with their quavers, but to listen to how fast the crotchets are going first. Keep the two rhythms going as long as necessary.

- You can also try different tempi (speeds).

- Even if pupils haven't previously heard the word syllable, it is an easy concept for them to learn, and playing the sounds may help them to understand it.

- In whole class situations it is useful to play an amplified instrument.

Activity 5: Arranging and Interpreting – Bear Dance

- Invite pupils to make decisions about the taps. What do they think sounds better – with the taps retained or not? Or should just some of the taps be retained, and if so, where? Try different versions, with the taps retained in different places. Ask pupils what they think.

- If playing the piece as an ensemble with all parts invite pupils to think of an introduction. This might be, for example, any, some or all of the parts playing bars 5 to 8. Invite pupils to consider which version sounds best.

Activity 6: Notation and Aural

Please see the pitch cards provided, on pages 20 to 23.

- Play card no. 2. Then look at card no. 1. Discuss how the last two notes of card no. 1 look different – that they are higher up the stave than the first two notes. Explain that if a note looks higher, it will sound higher (see **Top tips***). Given that the first two notes are both B, ask pupils what the last two notes might be. Having established that they are E, play the card. Ensure pupils have noted where the 'blob' on the note E is: in between the top two lines, i.e. in the top space. Work out and play the other cards.

- Play all four cards in a row. Shuffle them and play in a different order.

- Play a card and ask pupils to work out which one you played. Pupils need to work the notes out aurally, so ensure they can't see what string you are playing. Stand behind them to play, or turn your instrument around and pluck the strings. The individual who identifies the correct card first gets the chance to play a card for the rest of the group to identify. Ensure all have a go at this, so you can use the rule that if a pupil has already answered one, got it right and played, they should miss the next turn(s). This shouldn't take long with a small group, so no pupil should be waiting long. Again, ensure that pupils are working out the notes their friends are playing by aural rather than visual means. This works well for individual pupils too – just alternate who is playing and who is working out the answer.

Top tips:

- *Pupils should by now understand how the words 'higher' and 'lower' are used in music with regard to pitch. If not, return to the supplementary exercise after Activity 1: Echo Playing.

- For best results photocopy the notes onto card and laminate. For PDF versions of the pitch cards visit **www.musicwild.co.uk** and go to the **'Wild About Guitars'** tab: **'Pitch cards.'**

Practical considerations for WCET:

- You may want to photocopy the notes onto different coloured card – a different colour for each card. This ensures pupils can refer easily to a particular card, for instance, 'the yellow one' rather than 'the third one from the left' etc.

- Ask for volunteers to hold up the cards in a row. Choose pupils who you noticed have grasped the point well so that you can concentrate on checking learners who didn't initially understand.

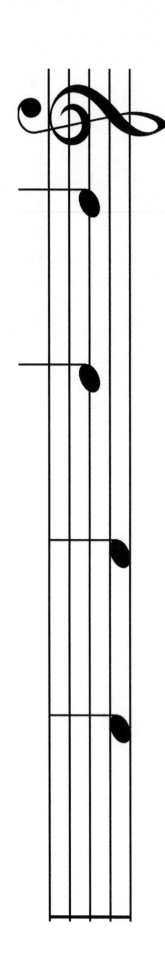

1

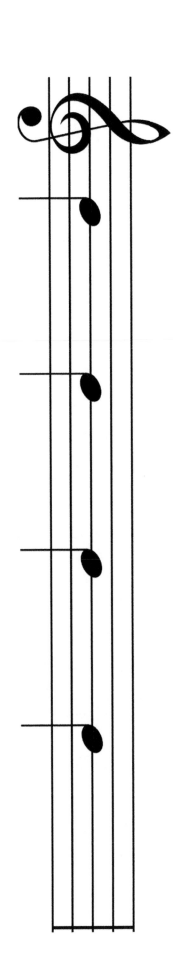

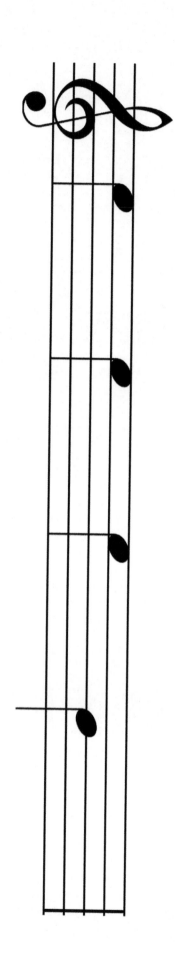

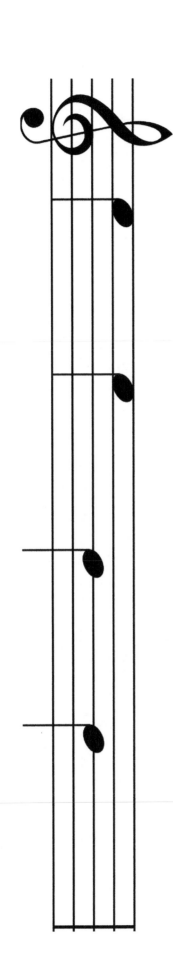

4

What Can We Do with Five Notes and a Two Finger Chord?

Activities use the notes **G A B D E**, and the chords **G** and **Am**

Activity 1: Echo Playing

see audio links '4a)i) and 4a)ii) Echo Playing 5 notes – GABDE'* and '4b)i) and 4b)ii) Echo Playing 2 chords – G and Am'*

- Play phrases of 2 bars in 4/4 using G A B D E for pupils to copy back.

- Start with the lowest note first and the next note up, then gradually move onto higher notes. Once you have reached the highest note come back down in a gradual way – E and D, then E, D and B and so on.

- Move step wise first, then, if pupils are managing this with ease, move onto phrases containing bigger intervals, such as G and B or G and D.

- For chords use the same process as in 'What Can We Do with Two Notes and One Finger Chords? Activity 1: Echo Playing' p.8.

For backing tracks visit:
www.musicwild.co.uk
and go to the
'Wild About Guitars' tab

* *tracks labelled i) include phrases for pupils to copy back, so facilitate home practice; tracks labelled ii) contain just the backing, giving the teacher more flexibility in lessons.*

Activity 2: Improvising - Riff and Rest, Riff and Play

see audio links '5a) Riff and Rest 5 Notes - GABDE' and '5b) Riff and Rest 2 chords – G and Am.'
A 'tutti' phrase is included.

- Follow the instructions for Riff and Rest, Riff and Play under 'What Can We Do with Two Notes and One Finger Chords?' p.9 but use all five notes in the phrase that everyone plays (i.e. G A B D E).

- Advise pupils that they need not use all five notes in their improvisations. It is best to choose just two or three, at least to begin with, and indeed simple improvisations are normally the most effective.

Point to Note:

Due to the notes pupils are choosing from, i.e. a pentatonic scale, all improvisations will sound good played simultaneously.

- For chords, use the same process as in 'What Can We Do with Two Notes and One Finger Chords? Activity 2: Improvising - Riff and Rest, Riff and Play' pages 9 and 10.

Top tips:

- Remember that the process can be broken into small chunks – perhaps a bullet point or two at a time - then returned to the following lesson.

- To help pupils remember which notes they can choose from you can

    a. Do the echo playing activity first

    b. Write each note as a letter on an A4 piece of paper and place the five pieces of paper in a circle on the floor where everyone can see them. Avoid putting the pieces of paper in a line, as pupils will be tempted to formulate improvisations with the notes exactly in the order they appear on the floor.

Activity 3: Working Out By Ear

- Sing the first two bars of Frère Jacques starting on G.

- Check that pupils recognise this tune. They may know different words, such as 'I Hear thunder.' You may wish to play the first two bars rather than sing, though remember to avoid giving pupils visual clues such as seeing which fingers/strings you use.

- Sing or play (giving no visual clues) just the first three notes. Ask pupils if they are all the same or if the notes go higher or lower.

- Having established that the notes go higher, say that the first note is a G (open string), and ask pupils to experiment to find the first three notes. Individual pupils can have a go, or all pupils can try together – quietly - so all have a chance of hearing themselves. When the correct notes have been found, ask all pupils to play the tune so far all together.

- Now sing or play the first four notes. Ask if the fourth was the same as the note before, higher or lower. Having established that it is lower, ask pupils to experiment again to find the right note.

- All play the correct version.

Top tips:

- When checking if pupils are familiar with a tune, be careful how you phrase the question. If you ask pupils 'do you know.......?' they may think you mean 'have you played this before?' Ask 'have you heard this tune before' and then play or sing it.

- If a pupil tries an incorrect note, help them to realise what might be wrong, so that that informs their next experimentation. For instance, a pupil might play the next string up (E), when trying to find the fourth note. Help them realise that this is a higher note and remind them that a lower note is what will sound correct. If they play a string which is incorrect but is lower, ask them if the note they tried is too low or not low enough.

- Once pupils have found the first four notes this can be turned into an ensemble activity. Ask them to play the fragment on a loop (over and over) whilst you play the tune in its entirety. Plot spoiler – they may fall into the trap of playing G A B G A B rather than repeating the G!

Activity 4: Learning a Tune Without notation – Bear Dance

(see audio link as referred to on p.14)

See score on p.16. Pupils will be playing line 3.

- Explain that for this two chords will be used - the ones they have been practising in other activities: A minor and G major.
- Establish that the first chord will be A minor.
- Ask pupils to turn around so they can't see you play. Invite them to put their hand up if and when they think you have changed to a different chord, and play them the first four bars.
- Having established the correct chords for the first four bars, all play.
- Repeat the procedure for the next four bars, and all play them.
- All play the first eight bars a couple of times.
- Play bars 9 to 12 with pupils turned around and ask them what the chords might be, having established that the first chord is A minor. They may be able to work out the whole four bars quite quickly now, or you may have to use prompting questions again, such as, 'where does the chord change?'
- Having established what the sequence is, all play those bars.
- Repeat for bars 13 to 16.
- All play bars 9 to 16 a couple of times.
- Play through the whole piece, verbally prompting chord changes if necessary.

Point to note:

- Pupils can be helped to memorise the chord sequences numerically - e.g. three A minor chords then one G major for the first four bars, and repetitions can be highlighted - e.g. bars 5 to 8 are the same as bars 13 to 16. However, it is better still, if pupils 'feel' where a chord needs to change, and this they will start to do if you play the melody alongside the chords as soon as possible. This may sound a little 'pie in the sky,' but I have witnessed the phenomenon in my own pupils, some of whom were as young as five!

Supplementary aural/rhythm exercise for differentiating crotchets and minims:

- Choose some words for: 4 crotchets; 2 minims; a minim and 2 crotchets; 2 crotchets and a minim. (See pages 15 and 17 for popular themes.) You might have chick-en tikk-a (4 crotchets), baked beans (2 minims), cheese sand-wich (minim + 2 crotchets) and fish and chips (2 crotchets + minim). Ensure the words will produce the desired rhythms when chanted, so for instance 'choc'late cake' only works for 2 crotchets then a minim, not a minim then 2 crotchets.

- Show pupils how to play the rhythms with the words. Use one of the notes or chords from the previous activities.

- Choose one of the rhythms, for example, cheese sand-wich, and play it without telling pupils which one you have chosen, i.e. they hear the notes but don't know which words they represent – they have to work it out. If a pupil answers correctly, they have a chance to choose one of the rhythms to play for the other pupils to work out. (In individual lessons they can play to you.) In small groups you can ensure that all pupils have a go eventually.

- To make the activity harder, play two rhythms consecutively, for example, cheese sand-wich + chicken tikk-a, or fish and chips + fish and chips.

Activity 5: Arranging and Interpreting – Bear Dance

- Once pupils know their part in Bear Dance invite them to try some different rhythms on the chords. You may find it useful to precede this activity with 'Activity 2: Improvising – Riff and Rest, Riff and Play' (chords). Encourage pupils to consider which rhythms work best.

- If playing the piece as an ensemble with all parts invite pupils to think of an introduction. This might be, for example, any, some or all of the parts playing bars 5 to 8. A rhythm created from the activity in the previous bullet point might work well for an introduction played by part three. Invite pupils to consider which version sounds best.

Activity 6: Notation and Aural

This is similar to Activity 6 in 'What Can We Do with Two Notes and One Finger Chords,' but uses a wipeable A4 white board with staves on (easily and cheaply available[2]) or an appropriate electronic device.

- Ask each pupil to write a group of four notes on the board. You may wish to use all five notes (GABDE) or any two or three, such as G and A or G, A and B.

- Label everyone's pattern of four notes: Mr Li's, Ayeesha's, Celina's etc. One person can write a pattern of four notes, the next person can name them, the next person can play them. Then move on, ensuring that every pupil has written, named and played.

- Play one of the patterns and ask pupils to work out which one you played. Ensure pupils can't see your strings/fingers, so stand behind them, or sing the pattern. Pupils need to use their ears to work it out, not their eyes. The individual who identifies the correct pattern first gets the chance to play a pattern for the rest of the group to identify. Ensure all have a go at this, so you can use the rule that if a pupil has already answered one, got it right and played, they should miss the next turn(s). With individual pupils, teacher and pupil can write two groups of four notes each.

Points to Note:

- By writing the notes down themselves, pupils achieve a thorough understanding of how one note is differentiated from another. It also helps you to check that they have understood which symbol represents which sound.
- When pupils first try this activity, you may wish to have the notes displayed in order somewhere, with relevant letters or fingerings written above. Pupils can refer to this to work out the patterns written down. However, ensure that this is just a transitional stage.

[2] For instance: www.musicroom.com/product/musch74085/wipe-clean-music-board-landscape-edition

What Can We Do with Eight Notes and a Three Finger Chord?

Activities use the scale of A natural minor (the Aeolian mode) – sometimes using the G below the key note, and include chords G, C and D7.

For backing tracks visit:
www.musicwild.co.uk
and go to the
'Wild About Guitars' tab

Activity 1: Echo Playing

see audio links '6a)i) and 6a)ii) Echo Playing – Scale of A natural minor'*

- Play phrases for pupils to copy back, as described in 'What Can We Do with Two Notes and One Finger Chords?' and 'What Can We Do with Five Notes and a Two Finger Chord?' pages 8 and 24.

Point to note

Phrases for pupils to copy back on the audio link (6a)i)) include the intervals featured in 'Learning a Tune Without Notation – Bear Dance' see p.35. This will help them when they come to that activity.

**tracks labelled i) include phrases for pupils to copy back, so facilitate home practice; tracks labelled ii) contain just the backing, giving the teacher more flexibility in lessons.*

Activity 2: Improvising a Melody

- Play through the A natural minor scale a few times to highlight what notes will be used in the improvisations. This activity is a good way to learn and reinforce the scale.

- Play a 2 bar 'questioning' phrase in 4/4, using notes from the A natural minor scale, and invite the pupil to answer with a 2 bar phrase. Emphasise that all notes of the scale need not be used, and indeed that improvisations using fewer notes are often more effective. After a few goes discuss the fact that some notes (particularly A) give a complete feel to the phrases, and some a questioning - or incomplete feel. You may wish to refer to the A as the key note or home note. Invite the pupil to have a few goes at attempting to finish on an A. In a small group pupils can take turns – play a questioning phrase for each pupil, and let each one have a turn at answering.

- The pupil is now going to play the 'question' and you the 'answer.' Count four beats in for the pupil. This is slightly harder for the learner, as they have to generate the raw material. However, pupils no longer need to finish on the key/home note. When you answer include aspects of the learner's phrase in yours. Point this out. It's useful for the pupil to understand that within a piece of music there will be variation but also some common factors. (In a small group take turns, as above.)

- Now the pupil is going to play both the 'question' and the 'answer.' Count the pupil four beats in. It's helpful to remind the learner that this is like a conversation. So far one of you has asked a question and one of you has answered. Now the learner is taking on both roles in the conversation.

- Ask the pupil to count themselves in, either out loud or with thinking voice, and to play a whole tune: question and answer. The learner is now equipped with all the tools they need to practise this at home.

Top tips:

- It may take a little while to get to the last bullet point, so until then just devote bite sized pieces to the activity in the lesson. A bullet point a week normally works well.

- If pupils continue to struggle with phrase length, return to the improvisation activity described in 'What Can We Do with Two Notes and One Finger Chords?' and 'What Can We Do with Five Notes and a Two Finger Chord?' pages 9 and 25 to help them internalise the appropriate number of bars.

- As an alternative to the whole scale, you may wish to use the notes featured in 'Learning a Tune Without Notation – Bear Dance' i.e. G A B C D E.

- Pupils can evaluate their tunes at home by recording themselves, using for instance, the camera on a phone.

Activity 3: Working Out By Ear

Melody: Frère Jacques

Having worked out the first four notes of Frère Jacques in 'What Can We Do with Five Notes and a Two Finger Chord?' pupils are now going to work out the whole tune, this time in C major. Apart from one, the notes sit conveniently inside a one octave A natural minor scale.

- Explain to pupils that they will now be working out the whole of Frère Jacques, this time starting on a C. Sing the tune, asking pupils to simultaneously sign the shape of the melody in a simple way – hand out in front, keeping it to the same level when a pitch is repeated, lifting higher when the pitch rises, and dropping lower when it falls. Sign with pupils to begin with.

- Repeat with you singing but not signing. Pupils continue to sign.

- Repeat *without* you singing. Pupils sign. (The tune is now only going on in their heads).

- If pupils are in a group, repeat but without them being able to see each other. You can ask them to face away from each other. This enables you to check that each pupil has understood, knows the tune, and can discriminate accurately between pitches.

- Ask pupils to sing the tune in their heads and think about what happens after the first four notes. From the earlier signing activity, they will have been reminded about the shape of the tune, so will probably answer fairly quickly that the first four notes are repeated.

- Use the questions from before to help pupils work out the rest of the tune, i.e.

  ...do notes stay the same or change?

  ...if they change, do they go higher or lower?

  ...by a lot or a little?

  Advise pupils to keep playing from the beginning, as to do otherwise can land them in the wrong key!

- At this point pupils can be asked to practise the tune at home, with just a reminder of what the first note is. Though they may forget some of the notes they have worked out, they should understand the process and be able to work them out again for themselves at home.

Top tips:

- When asking pupils to practise a tune which they are working out by ear, emphasise that they just need to experiment – the correct notes may well not be found immediately. Remind them not to go on to the next bit of the piece until they are satisfied each bit is correct, to avoid inadvertently changing key. Reassure them that this is a painstaking, sometimes slow process – it is not their own lack of ability that makes the process slow!

- When working out by ear with a group, and on more than just a short phrase or two, you can ask pupils to take it in turns to work out the notes - one pupil can work out the first few notes, then all play, then the next person plays from the beginning but works out the next bit as well, all play the notes so far, then onto the next pupil, and so on.

- A simple tune like Frère Jacques can be used constructively at different stages of pupils' learning. Choose an appropriate key to provide the required degree of difficulty, and to practise a particular learning point.

Point to Note:

- Jingle Bells is a great tune to work out by ear at Christmas time

Harmony: Happy Birthday to You

(see audio link '7 Working Out By Ear – Happy Birthday' for pupil practice)

- Make sure pupils can't see your fingers and strings. All sing the first two lines (up to the second 'to you') of Happy Birthday starting on D with you playing the chords.

- Explain that the first chord is G but that at some point chord D7 is needed to accompany the melody. Sing and play up to the first 'to you' at a steady speed, and ask pupils to put their hand up when they think the chord has changed.

- Play pupils answers, even if they are wrong, so that they can hear what they sound like – a wrong chord change won't correspond exactly to the version in their heads and will clarify what it is they are listening out for.

- When the correct version is found invite pupils to have a go at playing the chords all together with you singing the tune.

- Ask pupils what happens in the next short section regarding the chords: is it still D7 under the tune, or does it change back to G? Play both versions – just as far as the second 'Happy Birthday' – and ask pupils what sounds right. Pupils should of course still not be able to see your fingers and strings – they are working this out aurally.

- Once it has been established that D7 remains under the melody, explain that at some point the G chord returns. Sing the second phrase a few times, inviting pupils to simultaneously experiment quietly on their guitars, to work out where the G chord returns. When the correct answer has been found, all play the second phrase. If pupils struggle with this, use the process from the second bullet point, i.e. you play the chords and sing the tune, inviting pupils to put their hand up when they think the chord changes.

- All play the first two phrases whilst you sing.

- Pupils will be able to practise this at home with the audio link.

Top tips:

- It is sometimes useful to think about whether the music sounds 'finished' or not at the end of a phrase, and what chord achieves this effect, in other words, the tonic chord for a finished effect, the dominant chord for unfinished. A way of describing the effect of unfinished or finished is to compare it to finishing with a comma or question mark (unfinished), or a full stop (finished). This will help the pupil choose the appropriate chord.

Activity 4: Learning a Tune Without Notation – Bear Dance

(see audio link as referred to on p.14).

See score on p.16. Pupils will be playing line 2.

Preliminary exercises to familiarise learners with features from the tune:

- Repeat Activity 1: Echo Playing p.30. Be sure to use the range of notes and the intervals found in the melody.
- Play 2 bar rhythms taken from the melody (e.g. bars 5 and 6, or bars 7 and 8) on each of the first five notes of the A natural minor scale. Do this ascending and descending. Next, when arriving back to the key note, also play the rhythm on the G below, and then return to the key note.

Learning the tune – the first eight bars, or 'A' part.[3]

- Help learners to internalise the tune whilst still being musically involved by:
  - teaching pupils to tap the rhythm below on their instruments whilst you play the tune over the top. You may want to use words to remind them of the rhythms, as in 'What Can We Do with Two Notes and One Finger Chords?'
  - revising the chord progression from 'What Can We Do with Five Notes and a Two Finger Chord?' p.27 whilst you play the tune over the top.

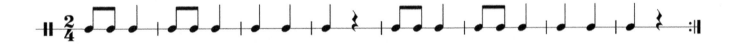

---

[3] In some genres, such as folk music, it is common to label sections of a tune with a letter name.

- Teach learners the tune, a fragment at a time. Sing or play the rest of the tune in between the fragments so that again, they will have many opportunities to hear and internalise it. To teach the fragments you can use a couple of strategies:

  — echo playing, so for instance, in bars 5 and 6 you can give the first note, play the bars and leave a gap for pupils to copy. You may need to do this is a few times, and you may also find it useful to use the questions from p.33 in Activity 3: Working Out By Ear

  — telling pupils the notes - particularly if time is pressing (e.g. if you have a concert coming up and/or you want to keep the pace flowing). Pupils may find the first two bars a little hard to work out due to the wide interval, so you may want to use this strategy here*.

  Once pupils can play the fragment, ask everyone to play it a few times on a loop to thoroughly internalise it. Invite learners to listen to the whole tune to hear where that fragment occurs. Play the tune several times with them joining in at the relevant point. To help learners understand where to join in, you can 'ghost' the rest of the melody (play quietly), indicate with body gestures where pupils begin to play (such as a nod of the head), or sing the rest of the melody.

  Use the same process to help pupils learn more and more fragments – see the suggested order below. Small fragments can be learnt separately, then put together with fragments already learnt, in the manner of assembling building blocks.

Learning the tune – the second eight bars, or 'B' part. [4]

- Use the same method as the first eight bars, with the same rhythm tapped on their instruments, and the chord progression from the 'B' part in 'What Can We Do with Five Notes and a Two Finger Chord?' p.27. See below for the suggested order to learn tune fragments. In this section it is very useful to encourage learners to spot repeated bits: bars 5 to 8 and bars 13 to 16; bars 9 and 11.

[4] In some genres, such as folk music, it is common to label sections of a tune with a letter name.

Top tips:

- *Learners will reap many benefits by working out pitches themselves, so avoid telling them the notes where possible.

- As well as discriminating between pitches, pupils will also need to remember successively large amounts of tune. To facilitate this, you can associate fragments with other tunes, point out the shape of the melody, or refer to expressive characteristics. So, for instance, bars 5 and 6 may remind pupils of a sad version of Twinkle, Twinkle Little Star. The notes in bar 7 might be said to go up steps two at a time then down two steps at a time. The first two bars sound quite declamatory – maybe they are calling the audience to listen.

- Unless pupils have access to a recording of the music it will be difficult for them to practise the material at home. If that is the case devote a comparatively small proportion of the lesson to learning the piece and return to it the following week. This will ensure you have enough time to spend on what **will** be practised for the following lesson.

- As pupils become more used to learning tunes without notation, the process will become quicker and more fluent, and some stages may even be omitted.

- Using the same principles, arrange your own pieces to suit your pupils.

Activity 5: Arranging and Interpreting – Bear Dance

- Ask pupils if there are any places where it would sound good to play the notes (particularly crotchets) staccato. Invite them to experiment.

- If playing the piece as an ensemble with all parts invite pupils to think of an introduction. This might be, for example, any, some or all of the parts playing bars 5 to 8. Invite pupils to consider which version sounds best.

- Pupils now know a tapped rhythm accompaniment. Would a performance be enhanced by including some or all of that?

Activity 6: Notation and Aural

- Repeat the activity as described in 'What Can We Do with Five Notes and a Two Finger Chord?' p.29. This time use the notes from A natural minor. It is good to use just a few at a time rather than the whole scale, e.g. A to E or E to A.

Appendix

Advice for teaching the activities online

At the time of writing *Wild About Guitars* many lessons are delivered online. This is largely due to covid-19 restrictions, though online teaching is sometimes the only way to deliver lessons if, for instance, pupils live in a remote area. Online teaching presents some challenges. I have outlined below how these might apply to the activities in this book, and suggested ways of dealing with any issues arising.

Echo Playing

On the whole there is not much problem with echo playing. You as the teacher will experience a gap after you have finished playing a phrase, but this won't be experienced by the pupil.
When using the supplementary exercise for differentiating pitch (p.9), there will be a gap between you moving pitch and the pupil moving their hand. This is easy to deal with as long as you expect it and don't try to fluctuate between pitches too quickly.

Improvising

— **Riff and Rest, Riff and Play (What Can We Do with Two Notes and One Finger Chords/Five Notes and a Two Finger Chord? pages 9 and 25).** This is not practical for online lessons, though pupils will be able to practise it at home with the online resource. This will benefit them in aiding the development of pulse and feel for phrase length. In lessons you can use the improvising a melody activity (see below). For this stage of playing, it is probably best to just ask pupils to improvise the answering phrase. They can still aim to finish on the 'home note' or tonic even with just two notes.

— **Improvising a Melody (What Can We Do with Eight Notes p. 31).** This is manageable, though there will be a gap experienced by the person playing the questioning phrase after they have finished – you in the first instance, but subsequently the pupil, so it is good to make them aware of this. Using the **Riff and Rest, Riff and Play** resource (see above) in their practice will ensure pupils are able to maintain a steady pulse and internalise the correct phrase length.

Working Out By Ear

This is absolutely fine online. However, asking pupils to sign lower/higher pitches whilst you sing the melody, or put up their hand for a chord change (as in **'What Can We Do with Eight Notes and a Three Finger Chord?' pages 32 and 34**) are problematic due to the time lag. Stick to making good use of questions, such as: 'does the tune stay on the same note, go higher or lower at this point?' For chord changes, the audio link will come in particularly useful.

Learning a Tune Without Notation

Generally, this is absolutely fine. Playing the tune whilst pupils play accompanying parts may be confusing for you due to the time lag, so you may want to mute them. In any case, pupils can make use of the audio resource to practice playing with other parts simultaneously. For working out chord changes in **'What Can We Do with Five Notes and a Two Finger Chord p.27** a question such as 'how many times did I play the same chord before changing to a different one' will work better than asking pupils to put their hand up. Learning the tune in the ways specified for **'What Can We Do with Eight Notes and a Three Finger Chord?' p.35** may be problematic due to the (normally helpful) strategy of getting pupils to play something whilst you play the tune. Instead, try to ensure pupils get a clear idea of the tune as a whole by playing it to them, inviting them to comment on any repeated bits and other structural details. Also ensure features of the tune are included in preliminary exercises so that they will be quickly spotted. Then make good use of echo playing, using short, then increasingly longer fragments.

Arranging and Interpreting

Activities for single parts of **'Bear Dance'** are fine, though of course those requiring ensemble playing are not.

Notation and Aural

This is fine, just ensure that you and the pupils are looking at equivalent things, i.e. the same note patterns in the same order. For **'What Can We Do with Five Notes and a Two Finger Chord/ Eight Notes and a Three Finger Chord?' pages 29/38** you may want to adapt that part of the activity which refers to pupils writing down their own notes.

Supplementary rhythm exercises

The aural/rhythm exercise for differentiating between crotchets and minims (p.28) is fine, but the exercise for subdividing the beat (p.17) is best saved for face-to-face lessons.